Keto Desserts Cookbook #2019

Mouth-Watering, Fat Burning and Energy Boosting Treats

Susan Carlsser

By reading this document, the reader agrees that under no circumstances are we responsible for any losses, direct or indirect, which are incurred as a result of the use of information contained within this document, including, but not limited to, errors, omissions, or inaccuracies.

Table of contents

Introduction

A meal is incomplete without a dessert. So, if you are getting severe craving for sweets on Ketogenic diet, what are you supposed to do as there is a restriction of sugars and carbs on a Ketogenic diet.

Yes, Ketogenic means that no sugar, no grains, no processed food but the good news is that you can still crave and satisfy your sweet tooth with your favorite dessert while being Keto. You can eat cakes, ice cream, tarts, pies, bars, ice cream, and any dessert when you go Keto.

In fact, even if you are a Keto-er, the fat burning desserts are way better than sugar filled ones.

Read on to know how exactly Keto desserts are beneficial for your health and how to keep yourself on track if you go overboard with sweetness.

Chapter1: Keto Desserts Basic

The ketogenic diet, or keto diet, is a high-fat diet that promotes a healthy lifestyle sans any carbs and sugar. A food with super-low or no amount of carbs gets the body into ketosis, which is the primary goal of the ketogenic diet. Ketosis is a metabolic process in which the body switch to fats to get energy when carbs reserves are finished. Following are some proven benefits of the ketogenic diet:

- Weight loss
- Clear skin
- Reduced inflammation
- Mental clarity and focused
- More energy
- Reduced cravings
- Reduce the risk of chronic and metabolic diseases

Let's go into some more details of the ketogenic diet.

So, when you consume high fat and low carb food, the body turns to utilized stored fats in the body. As a result, fat is broken down into simpler molecules called ketones which are transported to body cells to use as fuel. A great benefit of getting your body into ketosis is that when carbs are broken down into sugar, insulin hormone triggers craving and you feel unnecessarily hungry, while when carbs are limited, and fats are increased, these cravings are stopped and hence, your appetite gets into your control completely.

So, whatever you eat on a ketogenic diet, be it have carbs or sugar, just make sure that the body stays into ketosis process and don't spike its blood sugar level. Sugar is also a form of carbohydrate, and the amount of carbs allowed for a keto-er is about 50 grams or below this threshold per day. This amount includes refined sugar and all the sources of carbs.

So does this mean that you have to cut back on desserts? Absolutely not. Being on the Keto diet, you can still satisfy your sweet tooth and enjoy sweet treats. All you need to do is to prepare those desserts that don't bring your body out of ketosis. And, there are two keys to do this. Firstly, you need to choose keto-friendly ingredients that are high in fats to support ketone formation in the body. And, secondly, use a sweetener that doesn't spike blood glucose level to critical level. Luckily, there are many sweeteners available in the market that add flavor to your desserts, without increasing carbs and sugar in it.

- Stevia: This natural sweetener is nonnutritive, and this means it has no carbs or calories. Stevia is a great option to control and lower your blood sugar levels. It is available in both powdered and syrup form, but it is much sweeter than table sugar, therefore use less stevia quantity to achieve same sweetness – 1 teaspoon stevia for 1 cup sugar.

- Sucralose: This sucralose based artificial sweetener is indigestible and thus, provide no calories and carbs. Feel free to use this sweetener for any dessert except for those that require baking. Substitute it in the 1:1 ratio for most of the dessert recipes.

- Erythritol: It is a type of sugar alcohol that stimulates your taste buds which give you a taste of sugar. It can substitute sugar in a wide variety of dessert recipes, be it baking or cooking.

- Xylitol: This sugar alcohol is commonly found in gum and candies, and like other keto sweeteners, it has no carbs. Give a kick of flavor to your smoothies, shakes, tea, and coffee with this sweetener. Moreover, it also works well with baked desserts.

However, do add a little bit liquid when using xylitol as it absorbs moisture and increases dryness. Exchange xylitol in a 1:1 ratio with regular sugar.

- **Monk Fruit Sweetener:** As the name suggests, this sweetener is extracted from the monk fruit and thus, contain natural sugar. And, since this extract contains no sugar and calorie, it is an excellent option for a ketogenic diet. Use it anywhere in place of regular sugar.

You can also use fruits to add sweetness to your desserts such as:

- Strawberries
- Raspberries
- Blackberries
- Blueberries
- Lemon
- Lime
- Watermelon
- Cherries
- Peach
- Kiwi
- Cantaloupe
- Mandarin

Following are some sweeteners that are high in carbs, and you must avoid them.

- Honey
- Coconut sugar
- Maple syrup

- Agave nectar
- Dates

Here are some more tips that will help you satisfy your sweet tooth.

- It is normal to crave for sugar in the initial days of Ketogenic dieting. You will have temptation for sweet once in a while, and when this happens, Keto-friendly sweeteners can satisfy your sweet cravings without stalling your fat loss and maintaining the ketosis process in your body.
- Differentiate between the types of sweeteners that are available for the Ketogenic diet. There are three categories – natural sweeteners, sugar alcohols, and artificial sweeteners. Erythritol and stevia work just perfectly for any desserts without disturbing your insulin and blood sugar.
- Enhance your weight loss with Keto sweeteners. As mentioned before, sugar is also a form of carb and therefore, using them in an appropriate amount not only led to shedding weight, it also optimizes your health.

Chapter2: Benefits of Keto Desserts

So what's so great about low-carb desserts? Why should one have them?

Reason #1 – They contribute to weight loss. It turns out the limiting carbs in your desserts and emphasizing more on fats leads to more weight loss and improvement in overall health. The science behind this relates to the phenomenon of fuel for the body. For our body, carb is a go-to source for energy. And when it gets digested, it is converted into glucose and then burned for fuel. So, if you consume carb filled food and no other nutrients like fat and protein, the fat in your body lingers and adds on if you fail you burn all the carb reserve in your body.

Reason # 2 – When you restrict carb in your diet, the body switches to fat burning mood and create ketones which is another source of energy which the body can use. When this happens, the body enters into a metabolic state called ketosis which will result in the burning and reduction of stored fat in the body. Moreover, this process will keep you energetic without spiking your blood sugar levels.

Reason # 3 – It improves your overall health. Beyond the significant benefit of keto desserts which is weight loss, another advantage is substantial improvement in general health. It is proved scientifically that many ailments reduce significantly after eating low-carb consistently, like high blood pressure, coronary diseases, diabetes, epilepsy, dementia, and cancer.

With all these benefits, you might just forget about desserts, but the good news is that you don't have to.

Chapter3: Tips

Here are some tips if you mess up with your keto diet and ways to get back into a low-carb diet.

- Take notes: It's very common for keto to go off the rails and eat sugar or carbs. It might be fun in the beginning, but then the next day, you will feel serious discomfort and physically unwell like headache, stomach ache and inflammation. Moreover, it's quite easy to forget what you eat. Therefore, you need to remember your food and what you feel, and the best way is to write it down. So, make a habit of writing regularly about what you eat and how you feel about it. This could create a great significance in the future for you.

- Go for intermittent fasting: Intermittent fasting is widely recognized health practice in a Ketogenic diet. It's an opportunity for your body to deal with its toxic and junk you have eaten and detox it. Therefore, eat only when you feel really hungry and make sure that you next mean is Keto and don't forget to enjoy and savor it.

- Go Physical: You will fell a little low when you begin with exercise on a Ketogenic diet. It might hurt in the beginning, but afterward, you will feel much better. This doesn't mean that you have to do some high-intensity exercise. Just do some light exercise that raises your heartbeat for at least 15 minutes and breaks a sweat. A little exercise will clear your mind, improve digestion and control insulin level in the body.

- Sip water more: Being on Keto means that your body will lose lots of water. Although it is suggested to drink electrolyte drinks to provide your body with critical salts and keep it hydrated. What works more is simply drinking a cool liquid to make you feel energetic and on track. You can help yourself with herbal teas, without sweetener as well or something more flavorful to tickle your taste buds. Sip some warm bone broth; it will not fill your tummy without getting any carbs in it; it is satisfying and comforting as well.

- Sleep more: When your body switches to fats for energy, you could start losing your sleep as well. But you need to get a proper amount of sleep. Not getting enough sleep can disturb your Ketogenic lifestyle as it will prevent your body from functioning as it should be. Moreover, if you sleep enough, you are also preparing your body to handle the changes that come with implementing a Ketogenic lifestyle.

- Find a support group: Motivation is an essential factor to stay on the course. You need to promise yourself that you will follow the Ketogenic lifestyle with dedication. However, that promise you made in person can be easily broken. To avoid this, say it out loud in front of a support group or friends, you will feel that it's not easy to break. Therefore, find this support, you are numerous groups and forums online, and people there are very helpful and supportive, and they will also give you more ideas to help to keep you on track.

- Search some fun recipes: Another way to keep yourself excited is to turn the cooking and to eat Keto food into a fun activity. There are a number of websites and blogs with a lot of high-fat dessert recipes that are wonderful to make and satisfy your hunger.

In the following chapter, I have gathered some mouthwatering decadent desserts, from brownies, mousse, pies and frozen desserts, which will take your taste buds to gastronomical heaven. So, go into your kitchen and cook up some of your favorite desserts. Our Keto desserts incorporate a variety of Keto-friendly sugar substitutes. These sweeteners produce a sweet taste that is very close to sugar, but neither of these sweeteners converts into glucose or disturb ketosis. With all these tempting prospects, you should bear one thing in mind: just because the sweeteners are Keto friendly and have no calorie content, it doesn't mean that they can be consumed without limits. So, the best thumb rule is just to have sweet enough to tame your cravings.

Chapter4: Cake

Chocolate Cake

Servings: 8
Total time: 5 hours;

Nutrition Value:

Calories: 301 Cal, Carbs: 8 g, Fat: 27 g, Protein: 6 g, Fiber: 2 g.

Ingredients:

- 7-ounce dark chocolate, chopped
- 1/16 teaspoon salt
- 4 tablespoons swerve sweetener
- 4-ounce unsalted butter, cubed
- 4 eggs, separated
- ½ cup heavy cream

Method:

1. Set oven to 325 degrees F and let preheat.
2. Take an 8-inch cake pan, grease with butter and set aside.
3. Place chocolate and butter in a heatproof bowl and microwave for 45 seconds or more until melted.
4. Stir well, then add sweetener and cream and stir until thoroughly combined.
5. Beat in egg yolks, one at a time until combined.
6. Add salt into egg whites and beat at high speed until stiff peaks form.
7. Fold egg whites into prepared chocolate mixture until smooth, then spoon into prepared cake pan and smooth top with a spatula.
8. Place cake pan into the oven and bake for 45 minutes or until cake is set.
9. When done, cool the cake at room temperature and then chill for 4 hours in the refrigerator.

10. Slice and serve.

Caramel Cake

Servings: 12
Total time: 60 minutes;

Nutrition Value:

Calories: 388 Cal, Carbs: 7.6 g, Fat: 34.9 g, Protein: 9.5 g, Fiber: 3.4 g.

Ingredients:

- 2 1/2 cups almond flour
- 1/4 cup coconut flour
- 1/2 teaspoon salt
- 2/3 cup swerve sweetener
- 1 tablespoon baking powder
- 1/4 cup whey protein powder
- 1 teaspoon vanilla extract, unsweetened
- 1/2 cup unsalted butter, softened
- 4 eggs
- 3/4 cup almond milk, unsweetened

Method:

1. Set oven to 325 degrees F and let preheat.
2. In the meantime, take two 8-inch cake pans, line with parchment papers, then grease with oil and set aside.
3. Place flours in a bowl, add salt, baking powder, protein powder and stir well.
4. Place butter and sweetener in a large bowl and beat well until light and fluffy.
5. Beat in eggs, one at a time, and then beat in vanilla.
6. Add remaining ingredients and beat, one at a time, until combined and then divide the mixture between two cake pans.
7. Smooth the top with a spatula and bake for 25 minutes or until top is firm.

8. When done, cool the pan on wire rack for 15 minutes, then lift the parchment paper to cool cake completely.
9. Slice and serve.

Lava Cake

Servings: 1
Total time: 30 minutes;

Nutrition Value:

Calories: 173 Cal, Carbs: 4 g, Fat: 13 g, Protein: 8 g, Fiber: 2 g.

Ingredients:

- 2 tablespoons cocoa powder, unsweetened
- 1/16 teaspoon salt
- 2 tablespoons erythritol sweetener
- 1/4 teaspoon baking powder
- 1/2 teaspoon vanilla extract, unsweetened
- 1 egg
- 1 tablespoon heavy cream

Method:

1. Set oven to 350 degrees F and let preheat.
2. In the meantime, stir together cocoa powder and sweetener in a bowl until mixed.
3. Crack eggs in another bowl and beat until fluffy.
4. Add salt, baking powder, vanilla, eggs, and cream into cocoa mixture and stir well until incorporated.
5. Take a heatproof mug, grease with oil, then pour in prepared batter and bake for 10 to 15 minutes or until cake is set.
6. Cover the mug with a plate, hold it tightly and flip it upside down multiple times to slide cake to the plate.
7. Serve straightaway.

Butter Cake

Servings: 10
Total time: 60 minutes;

Nutrition Value:

Calories: 295 Cal, Carbs: 2 g, Fat: 30 g, Protein: 5 g, Fiber: 0 g.

Ingredients:

- 3 tablespoons coconut flour
- 1 teaspoon baking powder
- 1/4 cup erythritol sweetener
- 1/2 teaspoon vanilla extract, unsweetened
- 8 tablespoons unsalted butter
- 2 eggs

For Top Layer:

- 1/4 cup erythritol sweetener
- 1/2 teaspoon vanilla extract, unsweetened
- 50 drops liquid stevia
- 8 tablespoons unsalted butter
- 8-ounce cream cheese, softened
- 2 eggs

Method:

1. Set oven to 350 degrees F and let preheat.
2. In the meantime, take an 8-inch springform pan, grease it with oil and set aside until required.
3. Crack eggs in a large bowl, add vanilla and butter and whisk well.

4. Then add flour, baking powder and erythritol, whisk well and set aside until required.
5. Prepare top layer and for this, place butter and cream cheese in a bowl and beat using a hand mixer until creamy.
6. Add remaining ingredients and beat well until smooth.
7. Spoon the flour mixture into prepared pan, press and spread evenly, then pour in prepared butter-cream mixture and smooth the top with a spatula.
8. Place pan into the oven and bake cake for 30 to 35 minutes or until top is nicely brown.
9. When done, cool pan on wire rack completely.
10. Take out the cake from the pan, slice and serve.

Pound Cake

Servings: 16
Total time: 2 hours and 15 minutes;

Nutrition Value:

Calories: 254 Cal, Carbs: 4.4 g, Fat: 23.4 g, Protein: 7.9 g, Fiber: 1.9 g.

Ingredients:

- 2 ½ cups almond flour
- 1 ½ teaspoons baking powder
- ½ teaspoon salt
- 1 ½ cups erythritol sweetener
- 1 ½ teaspoons vanilla extract, unsweetened
- ½ teaspoon lemon extract, unsweetened
- ½ cup unsalted butter, softened
- 8 eggs
- 8 ounces cream cheese, chopped

Method:

1. Set oven to 350 degrees F and let preheat.
2. In the meantime, place sweetener and butter in a bowl and beat with an electric mixer until creamy and smooth.
3. Add cream cheese and continue blending until smooth.
4. Beat in extracts and eggs, one at a time, until incorporated.
5. Stir together flour, salt, and baking powder and beat in egg mixture, ¼ cup at a time, until very smooth.
6. Spoon the batter into greased loaf pan and place into the oven to bake for 1 to 2 hours or until inserted skewer into the center of the cake comes out clean.
7. When done, cool cake on wire rack completely and slice to serve.

Chocolate Zucchini Bundt Cake

Servings: 16
Total time: 1 hour and 10 minutes;

Nutrition Value:

Calories: 228 Cal, Carbs: 7.7 g, Fat: 20.8 g, Protein: 7.3 g, Fiber: 3.6 g.

Ingredients:

- 2 medium zucchinis, pureed
- 2 3/4 cups almond flour
- 1/2 cup cacao powder, unsweetened
- 1/2 teaspoon sea salt
- 1 1/3 cups erythritol sweetener
- 2 teaspoon baking powder
- 2 teaspoons vanilla extract, unsweetened
- 1/2 cup melted butter, unsalted
- 6 eggs

Method:

1. Set oven to 325 degrees F and let preheat.
2. Take a Bundt pan, grease with oil and set aside until required.
3. Stir together flour, cocoa powder, salt, sweetener and baking powder in a bowl.
4. Crack eggs in another bowl, add remaining ingredients and whisk well until smooth.
5. Pour this mixture into flour mixture and mix well until incorporated and smooth.
6. Spoon the batter into prepared Bundt pan and place into the oven.
7. Bake for 60 minutes or until an inserted wooden toothpick into the cake comes out clean.
8. When done, cool cake on wire rack completely and serve straightaway.

Lemon Poppy Seed Cake

Servings: 16
Total time: 1 hour and 30 minutes;

Nutrition Value:

Calories: 248 Cal, Carbs: 6 g, Fat: 23 g, Protein: 7 g, Fiber: 2 g.

Ingredients:

- 3 cups almond flour
- 3 tablespoons poppy seeds
- 2 teaspoons baking powder
- 1/2 teaspoon sea salt
- 1 cup erythritol sweetener
- 2 tablespoons lemon extract, unsweetened
- 2 teaspoons vanilla extract, unsweetened
- 3/4 cup unsalted butter, softened
- 4 eggs
- 3/4 cup sour cream

Method:

1. Set oven to 350 degrees F and let preheat.
2. Take a Bundt pan, grease with oil and set aside until required.
3. Place butter and sweetener in a bowl and beat with an electric beater until creamy.
4. Then beat in extracts, sour cream, and eggs, one at a time, until smooth.
5. Place flour in another bowl, add poppy seeds, baking powder, and salt and stir well.
6. Stir the flour mixture into butter mixture, ¼ cup at a time, until incorporated.
7. Spoon the batter into prepared Bundt pan and place into the oven to bake for 40 minutes or until top is dark golden brown.
8. Then cover the pan with aluminum foil and continue baking for 20 to 35 minutes or until an inserted toothpick into the cake comes out clean.

9. When done, let bake cool for 15 minutes and then turn it out to cool completely on wire rack.
10. Slice to serve.

Vanilla Cake

Servings: 12
Total time: 2 hours;

Nutrition Value:

Calories: 175 Cal, Carbs: 5 g, Fat: 15 g, Protein: 7 g, Fiber: 3 g.

Ingredients:

- 1 1/2 cup almond flour
- 1/4 cup coconut flour
- 1 teaspoon baking powder
- 1/4 teaspoon salt
- 2 scoops Vanilla Collagen Powder
- 1 teaspoon vanilla extract, unsweetened
- 1/4 cup melted butter, unsalted
- 3 eggs
- 1/4 cup sour cream
- 1 cup almond milk

Method:

1. Set oven to 350 degrees F and let preheat.
2. In the meantime, take an 8 by 4-inch loaf pan, grease with oil, then line with parchment paper and set aside.
3. Stir together all the dry ingredients in a large bowl until combined.
4. Crack eggs in another bowl, add vanilla and beat for 1 minute until fluffy.
5. Then beat in butter, sour cream and milk for 30 seconds until smooth.
6. Stir the mixture into flour mixture, in 2 to 3 batches, until well mixed and then let sit for 2 minutes.
7. Spoon the batter into prepared pan and bake for 50 to 60 minutes or until top is nicely golden brown and inserted toothpick into the cake comes out clean.

8. When done, let cake cool on wire rack for 15 minutes, then take it out to cool completely on wire rack and slice to serve.

Pumpkin Bundt Cake

Servings: 12
Total time: 1 hour and 30 minutes;

Nutrition Value:

Calories: 289 Cal, Carbs: 8 g, Fat: 26 g, Protein: 8.4 g, Fiber: 3.2 g.

Ingredients:

- 2 3/4 cups almond flour
- 2 teaspoons baking powder
- 1/2 teaspoons salt
- 1 1/3 cups Erythritol sweetener
- 2 teaspoons pumpkin pie spice
- 2 teaspoons vanilla extract, unsweetened
- 1/2 cup unsalted butter, melted
- 8.5-ounce pumpkin puree
- 6 eggs

Method:

1. Set oven to 325 degrees F and let preheat.
2. In the meantime, stir together all the dry ingredients in a large bowl until combined and set aside until required.
3. Place all the ingredients in another bowl and whisk until smooth.
4. Add this mixture into dry mixture and whisk well using a stand mixer until incorporated.
5. Spoon the mixture into a greased Bundt pan and place into the oven to bake for 60 minutes or more until top is nicely brown and inserted toothpick into the cake comes out clean.
6. When done, cool cake on wire rack for 15 minutes and then take out to cool completely.

7. Slice to serve.

Cheesecake

Servings: 12
Total time: 5 hours and 30 minutes;

Nutrition Value:

Calories: 517 Cal, Carbs: 28.8 g, Fat: 49 g, Protein: 12.2 g, Fiber: 21.3 g.

Ingredients:

For the Crust:

- 1 1/2 cups almond flour
- 1/4 cup monk fruit sweetener
- 4 tablespoons unsalted butter

For the Filling:

- 1 cup monk fruit sweetener
- 3/4 teaspoon vanilla extract, unsweetened
- 3 eggs
- 24-ounce cream cheese, softened
- 1/4 cup heavy whipping cream

Method:

1. Set oven to 350 degrees F and let preheat.
2. In the meantime, place butter in a heatproof bowl and microwave for 30 seconds or until melted.
3. Add remaining ingredients for the crust into melted butter, stir well until combined and add the mixture into 9-inch springform pan.
4. Press and spread the mixture evenly into the bottom of the pan, then place into the oven and bake for 8 minutes or until crust is nicely golden brown.

5. When done, remove crust from the oven and let cool on wire rack for 10 minutes, lower oven temperature to 325 degrees F.

6. Place all the ingredients for filling in another bowl and beat using a stand mixer until well combined.

7. Spoon this mixture into cooled crust, smooth the top with a spatula and place the pan into the oven.

8. Bake cake for 1 hour and 10 minutes or until set and inserted skewer into the center of the cake comes out clean.

9. Then cover the cheesecake with aluminum foil and chill in the refrigerator for 4 hours.

10. Slice and serve.

Chapter5: Bars

Chocolate Crunch Bars

Servings: 20
Total time: 10 minutes;

Nutrition Value:

Calories: 155 Cal, Carbs: 4 g, Fat: 12 g, Protein: 7 g, Fiber: 2 g.

Ingredients:

- 1 1/2 cups chocolate chips, stevia sweetened
- 1/2 cup monk fruit sweetener
- 1/4 cup coconut oil
- 1 cup almond butter
- 1 cup chopped almonds
- 1 cup chopped cashews
- 1 cup chopped pepitas

Method:

1. Take an 8 by 8-inch baking dish, line with parchment paper and set aside until required.
2. Place chocolate chips in a heatproof bowl along with sweetener, oil and butter and microwave for 60 seconds or more until melted.
3. Stir well until combined, then stir in almonds, cashews, and pepitas and spread the mixture evenly into the baking dish.
4. Place the baking dish into the freezer for 1 hour or more until firm.

Chocolate Chips Granola Bars

Servings: 16
Total time: 30 minutes;

Nutrition Value:

Calories: 307 Cal, Carbs: 10 g, Fat: 27 g, Protein: 6 g, Fiber: 6 g.

Ingredients:

- 1/3 cup goji berries
- 1/4 cup flax meal
- 1/4 cup chocolate chips, stevia sweetened
- 1/2 teaspoon ground ginger
- 3 tablespoons swerve sweetener
- 1/3 cup sukrin syrup
- 1 teaspoon cinnamon
- 1/3 cup pumpkin seeds
- 1/3 cup sunflower seeds
- 2 cups sliced almonds
- 1/2 cup walnuts
- 1/2 cup pecans
- 2 tablespoons melted butter, unsalted

Method:

1. Set oven to 350 degrees F and let preheat.
2. In the meantime, line a 13 by 9-inch baking dish with parchment paper and then grease with oil, set aside until required.
3. Place almonds in a food processor and pulse until chopped.
4. Tip almonds in a bowl, add remaining ingredients except for butter and syrup and stir well.
5. Then add butter and stir until mixed.

6. Add syrup and stir well and spoon the mixture into prepared baking dish.
7. Spread the mixture evenly, then cover with a wax paper and press granola with a flat-bottomed glass.
8. Place the baking dish into the oven and bake for 15 to 20 minutes or until edges begin to brown.
9. When done, cool the dish at room temperature for 10 minutes and then lift the parchment paper to take out granola.
10. Let granola cool completely, then cut into 16 bars and serve.

Peanut Butter Chocolate Bars

Servings: 8
Total time: 1 hour and 5 minutes;

Nutrition Value:

Calories: 246 Cal, Carbs: 7 g, Fat: 23 g, Protein: 7 g, Fiber: 3 g.

Ingredients:

For the Bars:

- 3/4 cup almond flour
- 1/4 cup Swerve Sweetener
- 1/2 teaspoon Vanilla extract, unsweetened
- 2-ounce unsalted butter
- 1/2 cup peanut butter

For the Topping:

- 1/2 cup chocolate chips, sugar-free

Method:

1. Place all the ingredients for bars in a large bowl, mix well and then spread evenly into a 6-inch pan.
2. Place chocolate chips in a heatproof bowl and microwave for 45 seconds or until melt.
3. Stir well, then spread chocolate on top of bars and refrigerate for 1 hour or more until thickened.
4. Cut into even pieces and serve.

Chocolate Fudge Protein Bars

Servings: 16
Total time: 1 hour and 10 minutes;

Nutrition Value:

Calories: 159 Cal, Carbs: 3.6 g, Fat: 14.8 g, Protein: 6.7 g, Fiber: 1.5 g.

Ingredients:

- 4 ounces sunflower seeds
- 2 scoops chocolate protein powder
- 1/2 teaspoon salt
- 3/4 cup swerve sweetener
- 3 ounces cocoa powder, unsweetened
- 8 tablespoons coconut oil
- 4 ounces tahini

Method:

1. Place all the ingredients in a blender or food processor and pulse for 2 to 3 minutes or until smooth, scraping the sides of the container.
2. Take a loaf pan, line with parchment paper, then spoon in prepared batter and spread evenly.
3. Place loaf pan into the refrigerator and refrigerate for 30 minutes or until firm.
4. Then cut into 8 bars and cut each bar to make 16 bars.
5. Continue freezing for 30 minutes or until hard and then serve.

Coconut Bars

Servings: 24
Total time: 40 minutes;

Nutrition Value:

Calories: 118 Cal, Carbs: 1.5 g, Fat: 12 g, Protein: 1 g, Fiber: 0.8 g.

Ingredients:

- 3 cups shredded coconut, unsweetened
- 1-ounce sugar-free chocolate
- 1/2 cup monk fruit sweetener
- 1/3 cup coconut cream, full-fat
- 4 tablespoons coconut oil

Method:

1. Place all the ingredients in a blender, except for chocolate, and pulse at high speed for 1 to 2 minutes or until sticky mixture comes together.
2. Take an 8 by 5-inch baking pan, line with parchment paper, then spoon in prepared mixture and press with a spoon to spread in the pan.
3. Place the pan into the refrigerator for 15 minutes or until firm and then cut into pieces.
4. In the meantime, place chocolate in a heatproof bowl and microwave for 30 seconds or more until melted.
5. Stir well, then fill into a plastic bag, pierce a hole with a needle and drizzle chocolate all over the coconut bars.
6. Return bars into the refrigerator for 10 minutes or until firm and then serve.

Protein Bar

Servings: 16
Total time: 1 hour and 5 minutes;

Nutrition Value:

Calories: 280 Cal, Carbs: 8 g, Fat: 24 g, Protein: 11 g, Fiber: 3 g.

Ingredients:

- 4 tablespoons chocolate chips, sugar-free
- ½ teaspoon pink salt
- 1 teaspoon monk fruit
- 2 scoops vanilla protein
- 1 cup of almond butter
- 4 tablespoons coconut oil, melted

Method:

1. Place all the ingredients in a bowl, stir well until mixed and add to a baking dish.
2. Spread the mixture evenly and place in freezer for 1 hour or more until firm.
3. Cut into bars and serve.

Lemon Bars

Servings: 8
Total time: 60 minutes;

Nutrition Value:

Calories: 272 Cal, Carbs: 4 g, Fat: 26 g, Protein: 8 g, Fiber: 3 g.

Ingredients:

- 1 3/4 cups almond flour
- 3 lemons
- 1 cup erythritol sweetener
- 1/2 cup unsalted butter, melted
- 3 eggs

Method:

1. Set oven to 350 degrees F and let preheat.
2. Place 1 cup flour, sweetener, and butter in a bowl and stir until mixed.
3. Spoon the mixture evenly into 8 by 8-inch baking dish, lined with parchment paper, and press and spread evenly.
4. Place baking dish into the oven and bake for 20 minutes.
5. When done, place baking dish on wire rack and cool for 10 minutes.
6. Zest one lemon, add to bowl, then add the juice of all lemons and add remaining ingredients.
7. Stir until combined, then spoon the mixture into the baking dish and spread evenly.
8. Place the baking dish into the oven to bake for 25 minutes or until set and top is nicely browned.
9. Slice and serve with lemon slices.

Nut Bars

Servings: 10
Total time: 1 hour and 10 minutes;

Nutrition Value:

Calories: 268 Cal, Carbs: 15 g, Fat: 22 g, Protein: 7 g, Fiber: 11 g.

Ingredients:

- ½ cup pumpkin seeds
- ½ cup sunflower seeds
- 1 tablespoon chia seeds
- 1/4 teaspoon salt
- 1/3 cup Fiber Syrup
- 1 teaspoon vanilla extract, unsweetened
- ½ cup shredded coconut, unsweetened
- 3 tablespoons almond butter
- 2 tablespoons coconut oil
- ½ cup almonds, sliced
- ½ cup walnuts, chopped

Method:

1. Take an 8-inch baking dish, line with parchment paper, then grease with oil and set aside until required.
2. Place vanilla, fiber syrup, butter and oil in a heatproof bowl and microwave for 30 seconds or more until melted.
3. Stir well, then add remaining ingredients and stir thoroughly until combined.
4. Spoon the mixture into baking dish, press and spread evenly and place into the freezer for 1 hour or until firm.
5. Slice and serve.

Samoa Cookie Bars

Servings: 16
Total time: 1 hour and 45 minutes;

Nutrition Value:

Calories: 216 Cal, Carbs: 6.5 g, Fat: 821.15 g, Protein: 2.9 g, Fiber: 3.1 g.

Ingredients:

For the Crust:

- 1 1/4 cups almond flour
- 1/4 teaspoon salt
- 1/4 cup swerve sweetener
- 1/4 cup unsalted butter, melted

For Chocolate Filling:

- 4 ounces unsweetened dark chocolate, chopped
- 2 tablespoons coconut oil

For Coconut Caramel Filling:

- 1 1/2 cups shredded coconut, unsweetened
- 1/4 teaspoon salt
- 1/2 cup swerve sweetener
- 1/2 teaspoon vanilla extract, unsweetened
- 3 tablespoons unsalted butter
- 3/4 cup heavy whipping cream

Method:

1. Set oven to 325 degrees F and let preheat.

2. In the meantime, prepare the crust and for this, stir together all the ingredients for crust until well combined.
3. Spoon the mixture into 8 by 8-inch baking pan, press and spread evenly and then place into the oven.
4. Bake crust for 15 to 18 minutes or until nicely golden brown and then cool on wire rack for 15 minutes.
5. Meanwhile, prepare the chocolate filling and for this, place chocolate and oil in a heatproof bowl and microwave for 30 seconds.
6. Stir well and then spread 2/3 of this mixture over the crust.
7. Prepare coconut filling and for this, place a skillet pan over medium heat and when hot, add coconut.
8. Cook for 2 to 3 minutes or until toasted and then set aside until required.
9. Place a large saucepan over medium heat, add butter and sweetener and cook for 3 to 5 minutes or until melted.
10. Bring the mixture to boil for 3 to 5 minutes or until golden and then remove pan from heat.
11. Stir in salt, vanilla, and cream and then stir in coconut.
12. Spoon and spread the mixture over the chocolate layer on crust and cool at room temperature for 1 hour.
13. Then cut into squares, drizzle with remaining chocolate filling and serve.

Chocolate Chip Bars

Servings: 24
Total time: 1 hour;

Nutrition Value:

Calories: 140 Cal, Carbs: 2.9 g, Fat: 13.5 g, Protein: 4.2 g, Fiber: 0.9 g.

Ingredients:

- 1/3 cup coconut flour
- 1 cup almond flour
- 1 cup chopped walnuts
- 1 1/2 teaspoons baking powder
- 1/2 teaspoon xanthan gum
- 1/4 teaspoon sea salt
- 2 cups swerve sweetener
- 1 cup chocolate chips, stevia sweetened
- 2 teaspoons vanilla extract, unsweetened
- 1/2 cup unsalted butter, softened
- 8-ounce cream cheese, softened
- 5 eggs

Method:

1. Set oven to 350 degrees F and let preheat.
2. In the meantime, take a 12 by 16-inch cookie sheet, line with parchment paper and set aside.
3. Place sweetener, vanilla, butter, and cheese in a bowl and whisk with a stand mixer until smooth.
4. Then beat in eggs, one at a time, until well incorporated and then gently fold in remaining ingredients until combined.

5. Spoon the mixture into prepared cookie sheet, spread evenly and place it into the oven to bake for 30 to 35 minutes or until nicely golden brown.
6. When done, let cookie bar cool completely and then slice to serve.

Chapter6: Pies and Tarts

Pumpkin Pie

Servings: 6
Total time: 1 hour and 10 minutes;

Nutrition Value:

Calories: 199 Cal, Carbs: 11 g, Fat: 17.2 g, Protein: 3.7 g, Fiber: 5.3 g.

Ingredients:

For Crust:

- 3 cups shredded coconut
- 1 tablespoon swerve sweetener
- 2 tablespoons coconut oil
- 2 tablespoons coconut cream

For Pumpkin Filling:

- 15 ounces steamed pumpkin
- 1/16 teaspoon salt
- 3 teaspoons cinnamon
- 2 teaspoons vanilla extract, unsweetened
- 2 teaspoons Collagelatin
- 3 tablespoons avocado oil
- 1/2 cup coconut cream
- 1/4 cup water

Method:

1. Prepare crust and for this, place coconut in a blender and pulse at high speed until very fine.
2. Add remaining ingredients for crust and pulse for 1 minute or until incorporated.
3. Take a 9-inch pie dish, line with parchment paper, then spoon in prepared coconut mixture and spread and press down using hands and then with a back of a spoon.
4. Place pie dish into the freezer and let it set.
5. In the meantime, prepare the filling and for this, stir together collagelatin and water and set aside until bloom.
6. Then add into a saucepan along with coconut cream and cook at low heat, frequently stirring until gelatin is dissolved completely.
7. Transfer this mixture into a blender along with remaining ingredients and pulse for 1 to 2 minutes or until smooth.
8. Remove pie pan from the freezer, spoon in prepared pumpkin mixture and smooth the top with a spatula.
9. Return pie pan into the freezer for 1 hour or more until set.
10. Slice and serve.

Key Lime Pie

Servings: 10
Total time: 1 hour and 10 minutes;

Nutrition Value:

Calories: 297 Cal, Carbs: 8 g, Fat: 28 g, Protein: 5 g, Fiber: 5 g.

Ingredients:

For Crust:

- ¾ cup almond flour, toasted
- 1/4 teaspoon salt
- 1/2 cup erythritol sweetener
- 1 teaspoon cinnamon
- 3 tablespoons coconut oil

For Key Lime Pie:

- 14-ounce avocado
- 2 tablespoons grated key lime zest
- 1/2 teaspoon salt
- 1/2 cup erythritol sweetener
- ¼ teaspoon key lime juice
- 8.8-ounce coconut cream, chilled

Method:

1. Place flour in a bowl, add remaining ingredients and stir until well combined.
2. Take a 9-inch pie dish, line with parchment paper, then spoon in prepared crust mixture and spread and press down using hands and then with a back of a spoon.
3. Place pie dish into the freezer and let it set.

4. In the meantime, place all the ingredients of lime pie in a blender and pulse for 1 to 2 minutes at high speed or until smooth.

5. Remove pie pan from the freezer, spoon in prepared key lime mixture and smooth the top with a spatula.

6. Return pie pan into the freezer for 1 hour or more until set.

7. Slice and serve.

Chocolate French Silk Pie

Servings: 1
Total time: 1 hour and 10 minutes;

Nutrition Value:

Calories: 394 Cal, Carbs: 13 g, Fat: 37 g, Protein: 9 g, Fiber: 8 g.

Ingredients:

For the Crust:

- 1 ¾ tablespoon almond flour
- 1/16 teaspoon salt
- 3 teaspoons Swerve sweetener
- 2 teaspoons cocoa powder
- 3 teaspoons melted butter
- 1/8 teaspoon instant coffee

For the Filling:

- ½ of a medium avocado
- ¾ tablespoon cocoa powder
- 1/8 teaspoon salt
- 3 tablespoons Swerve sweetener
- 1/2 teaspoon vanilla extract, unsweetened
- 1/4 teaspoon instant coffee
- 1/3 cup coconut milk, full-fat and unsweetened

Method:

1. Place flour in a bowl, add remaining ingredients and stir until well combined.

2. Take a 4 ½-inch pie dish, line with parchment paper, then spoon in prepared crust mixture and spread and press down using hands and then with a back of a spoon.
3. Place pie dish into the freezer and let it set.
4. In the meantime, place all the ingredients of filling in a blender and pulse for 1 to 2 minutes at high speed or until smooth.
5. Remove pie pan from the freezer, spoon in prepared filling and smooth the top with a spatula.
6. Return pie pan into the freezer for 1 hour or more until set.
7. Slice and serve.

Lemon Meringue Pie

Servings: 6
Total time: 4 hours and 30 minutes;

Nutrition Value:

Calories: 217 Cal, Carbs: 9 g, Fat: 19 g, Protein: 7 g, Fiber: 3 g.

Ingredients:

For the Crust:

- ½ cup almond flour
- ½ cup coconut flour
- 2 tablespoons Swerve sweetener
- 1 teaspoon vanilla extract, unsweetened
- 2 teaspoons arrowroot
- ½ cup unsalted butter, cut in small cubes
- 2 eggs

For the Filling:

- 1 tablespoon arrowroot
- ¼ teaspoon salt
- 1 ¼ cups Swerve sugar
- 1 envelope of gelatin
- 3 tablespoons unsalted butter
- 2 teaspoons grated lemon zest
- ½ cup lemon juice
- 1 ¼ cup water
- 4 egg yolks, beaten

For the Meringue:

- ½ cup Swerve sugar
- 4 egg whites
- ½ teaspoon cream of tartar

Method:

1. Set oven to 350 degrees F and let preheat.
2. In the meantime, place all the ingredients for crust in a food processor and pulse for 10 to 12 minutes or until crumbly.
3. Take a 9-inch pie dish, line with parchment paper, then spoon in prepared crust mixture and spread and press down using hands and then with a back of a spoon.
4. Place pie dish into the oven and bake for 10 to 12 minutes or until nicely brown.
5. In the meantime, prepare the filling and for this, place a small saucepan over medium heat, and add salt, sweetener, gelatin, and water.
6. Stir well until gelatin dissolves and bring the mixture to boil.
7. Then boil for 1 minute, slowly pour in egg yolks and continue cooking until thickened.
8. Whisk in lemon juice and zest, and butter, then remove the pan from heat and set aside.
9. Prepare meringue and for this, place egg whites in a bowl and whip at low speed until foamy.
10. Then slowly whisk in sugar until stiff peaks form.
11. When pie crust is done, spoon filling into it and top completely with prepared meringue.
12. Return pie into the oven and bake for 30 minutes or until meringue is lightly browned.
13. When done, cool pie at room temperature for 1 hour and then in the refrigerator for 3 hours.
14. Slice and serve.

Berries and Mascarpone Cream Tart

Servings: 6
Total time: 30 minutes;

Nutrition Value:

Calories: 237 Cal, Carbs: 5 g, Fat: 22 g, Protein: 5 g, Fiber: 2 g.

Ingredients:

For the Tart Crust:

- 2 1/4 cups almond flour
- 1/4 teaspoon sea salt
- 1/4 cup erythritol sweetener
- 5 tablespoons melted butter

For the Mascarpone Cream:

- 2 tablespoons erythritol sweetener
- 1/4 teaspoon lemon zest
- 1 teaspoon vanilla extract, unsweetened
- 6-ounce mascarpone cheese, full-fat
- 1/3 cup heavy cream

For Garnishing:

- 6 raspberries
- 3 strawberries, halved
- 6 blueberries
- 6 blackberries

Method:

1. Set oven to 350 degrees F and let preheat.
2. In the meantime, grease six tart pan, each about 4-inch, and set aside.
3. Prepare the crust and for this, stir together all the ingredients for crust until incorporated.
4. Divide evenly between the prepared tart pan and press down evenly, down the walls and bottom.
5. Use a fork to make holes in the dough and then place pan into the oven to bake for 8 to 10 minutes or until nicely golden brown.
6. When done, place tart pans on wire rack and cool completely.
7. Meanwhile, prepare mascarpone cream and for this, place cheese in a bowl, then add sweetener and beat with an electric mixer for 2 minutes at low speed.
8. Slowly beat in cream, then increase mixer speed to medium and continue beating for 30 to 60 seconds or until thick.
9. Then beat in lemon zest and vanilla until mixed.
10. Spoon the filling into prepared tarts, smooth with top and top with berries.
11. Serve straightaway.

Lemon Curd Tart with Blackberries

Servings: 12
Total time: 35 minutes;

Nutrition Value:

Calories: 216 Cal, Carbs: 10.6 g, Fat: 19.9 g, Protein: 7.7 g, Fiber: 5.7 g.

Ingredients:

- 12-ounce blackberries
- 1 tablespoon sliced almonds
- 1 cup lemon curd, chilled

For Pie Crust:

- 1 ½ cup almond flour
- ½ cup coconut flour
- 4 tablespoons erythritol sweetener
- 4 tablespoons unsalted butter, chilled
- 2 eggs

Method:

1. Set oven to 350 degrees F and let preheat.
2. In the meantime, prepare the crust and for this, place all the ingredients for crust in a large bowl, stir well and knead for 3 minutes or more until dough comes together.
3. Take two 9-inch tart pan and grease with oil and line with a parchment sheet.
4. Divide dough into two portions, add each portion to the tart pan and spread evenly throughout the pan.
5. Place pan into the oven and bake for 15 minutes or until crusts are nicely browned.

6. Let baked crusts cool completely, then add lemon curd in it and cover with berries and lemon slices.
7. Serve straightaway.

Cheesecake Tarts

Servings: 12
Total time: 1 hour and 30 minutes;

Nutrition Value:

Calories: 196 Cal, Carbs: 14 g, Fat: 16 g, Protein: 9 g, Fiber: 1.2 g.

Ingredients:

For the Crust:

- ¾ cup almond flour
- 3 tablespoons unsalted butter, melted

For the Filling:

- ¼ teaspoon salt
- ¼ cup erythritol sweetener
- 1 tablespoon lemon juice
- 1 teaspoon vanilla extract, unsweetened
- 12-ounce cream cheese, softened
- 1 egg

For the Toppings:

- ¼ cup blueberries
- ¼ cup strawberry jam, sugar-free

Method:

1. Set oven to 350 degrees F and let preheat.
2. In the meantime, prepare the crust and for this stir together flour and butter until crumbly mixture comes together.

3. Take 12 cups muffin pan, line each tin with a paper cup, then add 1 to 2 teaspoons almond flour mixture and spread evenly on the bottom.
4. Place muffin pan into the oven and bake for 5 to 8 minutes or more until golden brown.
5. When done, transfer muffin pan on wire rack and let cool completely.
6. In the meantime, prepare the filling and for this, place cream cheese into the oven and beat with an electric beater at high speed until soft peaks form.
7. Beat in egg, sweetener, lemon juice, vanilla, and salt until mixed well and spoon the filling into cooled crusts.
8. Return muffin pan into the oven and bake for 20 minutes or until set.
9. When done, let muffins cool at room temperature for 10 minutes and then top each muffin with 1 teaspoon jam.
10. Top with berries, chill in refrigerator and serve.

Lemon Coconut Custard Pie

Servings: 8
Total time: 55 minutes;

Nutrition Value:

Calories: 209 Cal, Carbs: 6 g, Fat: 19 g, Protein: 3 g, Fiber: 3 g.

Ingredients:

- ¼ cup coconut flour
- 4 ounces shredded coconut, unsweetened
- ¾ cup erythritol sweetener
- ¾ teaspoon baking powder
- 1 teaspoon lemon zest
- 1 teaspoon vanilla extract, unsweetened
- ½ teaspoon lemon extract, unsweetened
- 2 tablespoons unsalted butter, melted
- 2 eggs
- 1 cup coconut milk, unsweetened and full-fat

Method:

1. Set oven to 350 degrees F and let preheat.
2. In the meantime, take a 9-inch pie dish, grease with oil and set aside.
3. Crack eggs in a bowl, add remaining ingredients except for coconut and stir well until combined.
4. Then fold in coconut and spoon the mixture into a pie dish, smooth the top with a spatula.
5. Place pie dish into the oven and bake for 40 to 45 minutes or until pie is set and its edges and top is nicely golden brown.
6. When done, let pie cool on wire rack completely.
7. Slice to serve.

Chapter7: Cookies

Pecan Pie Cookies

Servings: 23
Total time: 40 minutes;

Nutrition Value:

Calories: 167 Cal, Carbs: 5 g, Fat: 16 g, Protein: 5 g, Fiber: 4 g.

Ingredients:

- 1 cup almonds
- 1/4 cup chia seeds
- 1/4 cup chocolate chips, unsweetened
- 1 cup pecans, and more for topping
- 1 cup candied pecans, sugar-free
- 1/2 cup erythritol sweetener
- 1 cup almond butter
- 1/4 cup coconut milk

Method:

1. Place all pecans and almonds in a food processor and pulse for 1 minute or more until crumbled.
2. Add remaining ingredients and blend until thick mixture comes together, add more milk if the mixture is crumbly.
3. Tip the mixture in a large bowl, then shape into 23 cookie balls and place on a baking tray, lined with parchment paper.
4. Top cookies with more pecans and chill in the refrigerator for 30 minutes or until firm.
5. Serve straightaway.

Chocolate Cookies

Servings: 20
Total time: 55 minutes;

Nutrition Value:

Calories: 98 Cal, Carbs: 5 g, Fat: 8 g, Protein: 4 g, Fiber: 3 g.

Ingredients:

- 3/4 cup coconut flour
- 1/2 cup monk fruit sweetener
- 2 cups Nutella, low-carb

Method:

1. Place all the ingredients in a large bowl and stir well until thick batter comes together.
2. Shape the mixture into 20 cookie balls and place on a baking tray lined with parchment paper.
3. Place the baking tray into the refrigerator and chill for 45 minutes or until firm.
4. Serve straightaway.

Peanut Butter Cookies

Servings: 4
Total time: 40 minutes;

Nutrition Value:

Calories: 282 Cal, Carbs: 6 g, Fat: 21 g, Protein: 19 g, Fiber: 4 g.

Ingredients:

- 6 tablespoons coconut flour
- 2 tablespoon chocolate chips, unsweetened
- 1 tablespoon monk fruit sweetener
- ¾ cup peanut butter

Method:

1. Place butter in a bowl, add sweetener and stir well until mixed.
2. Then add coconut flour and stir well until thick dough comes together, add more flour if the batter is too thin or more liquid if the batter is too thick.
3. Shape dough into four balls and place on a plate, lined with parchment paper.
4. Press cookie balls lightly, top with chocolate chips and place into refrigerator for 30 minutes or until firm.
5. Serve straightaway.

Coconut Cookies

Servings: 40
Total time: 40 minutes;

Nutrition Value:

Calories: 40 Cal, Carbs: 2 g, Fat: 4 g, Protein: 1 g, Fiber: 2 g.

Ingredients:

- 1 cup chocolate chips, unsweetened
- 1 cup almond flour
- 3 cups shredded coconut, unsweetened
- 3/4 cup monk fruit sweetener
- 1/4 cup coconut milk, unsweetened and full-fat

Method:

1. Place all the ingredients in a blender and pulse at high speed for 1 to 2 minutes or until incorporated and thick batter comes together.
2. Shape mixture into 40 cookie balls and place on a large baking tray, lined with parchment paper.
3. Place the baking tray into the refrigerator for 30 minutes until cookies are firm.
4. Serve straightaway.

Coconut Snowball Cookies

Servings: 40
Total time: 40 minutes;

Nutrition Value:

Calories: 40 Cal, Carbs: 2 g, Fat: 4 g, Protein: 1 g, Fiber: 2 g.

Ingredients:

- 4 cups shredded coconut, unsweetened
- 1/4 cup monk fruit sweetener
- 1/4 teaspoon vanilla extract, unsweetened
- 1/2 cup coconut milk, unsweetened and full-fat

Method:

1. Place coconut in a blender and pulse for 1 to 2 minutes at high speed or until fine texture, don't over blend.
2. Add sweetener and milk and continue blending for 1 minute or until thick batter comes together.
3. Tip the mixture into a large bowl and shape into 40 small cookie balls.
4. Place cookie balls on a baking tray lined with parchment paper, and press lightly into a cookie shape.
5. Sprinkle with coconut and place into refrigerator for 30 minutes until firm.
6. Serve straightaway.

Peppermint Chocolate Cookies

Servings: 30
Total time: 40 minutes;

Nutrition Value:

Calories: 89 Cal, Carbs: 4.4 g, Fat: 7 g, Protein: 2.2 g, Fiber: 2 g.

Ingredients:

- 1 1/2 cup almond flour
- 1/4 cup coconut flour
- 1 cup mixed chocolate chips, divided
- 2 tablespoons cocoa powder
- 1/8 teaspoon sea salt
- 2 tablespoons erythritol sweetener
- 1/4 cup monk fruit sweetener
- 1 scoop chocolate protein powder
- 1/2 teaspoon peppermint extract, unsweetened
- 1/2 cup cashew butter
- Coconut milk as needed

Method:

1. Place flours in a large bowl, add cocoa powder, salt, sweetener, and protein powder and stir well, set aside until required.
2. Place butter in a heatproof bowl, add monk fruit sweetener and microwave for 45 seconds or until butter is melt.
3. Stir well until combined, then stir in mint extract and add to flour mixture.
4. Mix well until crumbly batter comes together and then slowly stir in milk until thick batter comes together.
5. Fold in half of the chocolate chips, then shape mixture into small cookie balls and place on a cookie sheet lined with parchment paper.

6. Press each cookie ball slightly, top with remaining chocolate chips and refrigerate for 30 minutes or more until firm.
7. Serve straightaway.

White Chocolate Cranberry Cookies

Servings: 30
Total time: 40 minutes;

Nutrition Value:

Calories: 45.5 Cal, Carbs: 1.47 g, Fat: 3.6 g, Protein: 1.7 g, Fiber: 1.2 g.

Ingredients:

- 1/4 cup dried cranberries, unsweetened
- 3/4 cup coconut flour
- 1 scoop whey protein powder
- 1/16 teaspoon sea salt
- 1/2 cup monk fruit sweetener
- 1/4 cup erythritol sweetener
- 1/2 cup cashew butter
- 1/4 cup white chocolate chips, unsweetened
- Almond milk, as needed

Method:

1. Place flour in a large bowl, add protein powder, salt, and erythritol and stir until mixed.
2. Add butter and monk fruit sweetener and stir well until the crumbly mixture comes together.
3. Fold in chocolate and berries until incorporated and then slowly mix milk until thick batter comes together.
4. Shape the mixture into small cookie balls, then place them on a cookie sheet lined with parchment paper and press each cookie ball slightly.
5. Place cookie sheet into the refrigerator for 30 minutes or more until firm.
6. Serve straightaway.

Shortbread Cookies

Servings: 16
Total time: 35 minutes;

Nutrition Value:

Calories: 126 Cal, Carbs: 2 g, Fat: 12 g, Protein: 3 g, Fiber: 1 g.

Ingredients:

- 2 cups almond flour
- 1/16 teaspoon salt
- 1/3 cup erythritol sweetener
- 1 teaspoon vanilla extract, unsweetened
- 1/2 cup softened butter, unsalted
- 1 egg

Method:

1. Set oven to 350 degrees F and let preheat.
2. In the meantime, place flour in a large bowl, add salt, sweetener, and vanilla and mix well.
3. Add butter and rub until thoroughly combined.
4. Add egg, mix well and then shape mixture into 16 cookie balls.
5. Place cookie balls on a parchment lined cookie sheet and place into the oven.
6. Bake cookies for 15 to 25 minutes or until edges are nicely brown and cookies are firm.
7. When done, cool the cookies on a wire rack and then serve.

Chapter8: Candy and Confections

Lemon Drop Gummies

Servings: 4
Total time: 3 hours and 5 minutes;

Nutrition Value:

Calories: 15 Cal, Carbs: 1 g, Fat: 0 g, Protein: 3 g, Fiber: 0 g.

Ingredients:

- 2 tablespoons gelatin powder
- 2 tablespoons erythritol sweetener
- 1/4 cup lemon juice
- 1 tablespoon water

Method:

1. Place a small saucepan over medium heat, add lemon juice and water and cook for 2 minutes or until hot.
2. Then stir in gelatin and sweetener until gelatin is dissolve.
3. Divide the mixture evenly into 4 silicone molds and place in freezer for 2 to 3 hours or until firm.
4. Serve straightaway.

Chocolate Almond Clusters

Servings: 17
Total time: 50 minutes;

Nutrition Value:

Calories: 96 Cal, Carbs: 2 g, Fat: 8.4 g, Protein: 2 g, Fiber: 3.3 g.

Ingredients:

- 3 ounces dark chocolate, chopped
- 1 cup almonds
- 1 tablespoon erythritol sweetener
- 2 ounces butter, unsalted

Method:

1. Place chocolate and butter in a heatproof bowl and microwave for 45 seconds or more until melted.
2. Stir in almonds until combined and refrigerate for 10 to 15 minutes or until thick.
3. Then place tablespoons of almond-chocolate mixture onto baking sheets and chill in the freezer for 30 minutes or more until firm.
4. Serve straightaway.

Chocolate Coconut Candies

Servings: 20
Total time: 55 minutes;

Nutrition Value:

Calories: 240 Cal, Carbs: 5 g, Fat: 25 g, Protein: 2 g, Fiber: 1 g.

Ingredients:

Coconut Candies:

- 3 tablespoons swerve sweetener
- 1/2 cup shredded coconut, unsweetened
- 1/2 cup coconut butter
- 1/2 cup avocado oil

Chocolate Topping:

- 1-ounce chocolate, unsweetened
- 1/4 cup swerve sweetener
- 1/4 cup cocoa powder
- 1/4 teaspoon vanilla extract, unsweetened
- 1.5 ounces cocoa butter

Method:

1. Line 20 mini muffin pans with paper liners and set aside.
2. Place a saucepan over low heat, add butter and oil and cook for 3 minutes or more until melted, stirring frequently.
3. Then stir in coconut and sweetener until combined and divide the mixture evenly between prepared muffin cups.
4. Place muffin cups into the freezer and chill for 30 minutes or more until firm.

5. In the meantime, prepare chocolate topping and for this, place butter and chocolate in a bowl and microwave for 45 seconds or more until melted.
6. Stir well, add remaining ingredients for topping and stir until combined.
7. When candies are firm, remove from freezer and spoon prepared chocolate topping on them.
8. Let chocolate coated candies sit for 15 minutes at room temperature.
9. Serve straightaway.

Chocolate Truffles

Servings: 12
Total time: 2 hours and 5 minutes;

Nutrition Value:

Calories: 111 Cal, Carbs: 4.5 g, Fat: 10 g, Protein: 1.5 g, Fiber: 3 g.

Ingredients:

- 2 medium avocados, pitted and peeled
- 1/2 cup chopped pecans
- 1/2 cup cocoa powder, unsweetened
- 1 tablespoon swerve sweetener
- 2 tablespoons chocolate flavored syrup
- 2 tablespoons avocado oil
- 2 tablespoons heavy whipping cream

Method:

1. Place all the ingredients except for pecans in a blender and pulse at high speed for 1 to 2 minutes or until combined.
2. Tip the mixture in a bowl and chill in the refrigerator for 1 hour or more until firm.
3. Then shape the mixture into 12 balls, each about 1-inch in size, and roll in the pecans.
4. Return balls into the refrigerator and chill for 1 hour or until firm.
5. Serve straightaway.

Lemon Lime Coconut Candy

Servings: 20
Total time: 1 hour and 10 minutes;

Nutrition Value:

Calories: 136 Cal, Carbs: 2 g, Fat: 13.7 g, Protein: 1 g, Fiber: 2 g.

Ingredients:

- 1/2 cup shredded coconut, unsweetened
- 1 lemon, zested and juiced
- 2 limes, zested and juiced
- 1/8 teaspoon sea salt
- 1 teaspoon liquid stevia
- 1 teaspoon vanilla extract, unsweetened
- 1/4 teaspoon lemon extract, unsweetened
- 1/4 teaspoon lime extract, unsweetened
- 1 cup coconut butter
- 1/2 cup coconut oil

Method:

1. Place a small saucepan over low heat, add coconut butter and oil and cook for 2 to 3 minutes or until melts.
2. Then whisk in remaining ingredients until smooth and spread the mixture into the glass dish.
3. Place dish into the freezer for 1 hour or until firm and then cut into chunks.
4. Serve straight away or store in the freezer.

Peppermint Bark

Servings: 12
Total time: 5 minutes;

Nutrition Value:

Calories: 131 Cal, Carbs: 3.7 g, Fat: 13.8 g, Protein: 0.5 g, Fiber: 1.7 g.

Ingredients:

For Dark Chocolate Layer:

- 1/2 teaspoon peppermint extract
- 4 ounces dark chocolate, chopped
- 1/2-ounce cocoa butter

For White Chocolate Layer:

- 3 tablespoons swerve sweetener
- 1/2 teaspoon peppermint extract, unsweetened
- 2 ounces cocoa butter
- 1/4 cup coconut oil

Method:

1. Prepare dark chocolate layer and for this, place chocolate and cocoa butter in a heatproof bowl.
2. Microwave the mixture for 45 seconds or more until melted and then stir in peppermint extract.
3. Take a baking sheet, line with parchment paper, then place 24 mini muffin cups and evenly spoon melted chocolate into it, spreading chocolate into the corner.
4. Place muffin cups into the freezer and chill for 30 minutes or more until set and firm.

5. In the meantime, prepare white chocolate layer and for this, place cocoa butter and oil in a heatproof bowl and microwave for 30 seconds or more until melted.
6. Stir well until smooth and then whisk in sweetener and extract until combined.
7. Spread the mixture over dark chocolate layer and freeze for another 15 to 20 minutes or until set.
8. Serve straight away or store in the freezer.

Peanut Butter Cups

Servings: 12
Total time: 1 hour and 40 minutes;

Nutrition Value:

Calories: 200 Cal, Carbs: 6.2 g, Fat: 19 g, Protein: 2.9 g, Fiber: 3.6 g.

Ingredients:

- 4 ounces dark chocolate, sugar-free
- 1/3 cup swerve sweetener
- 1/2 teaspoon vanilla extract, unsweetened
- 1/2 cup peanut butter
- 3 ounces cacao butter, chopped
- 1/4 cup butter, unsalted

Method:

1. Place butter in a small saucepan, place over low heat and stir until smooth.
2. Then stir in sweetener and vanilla until well combined.
3. Line 12 mini muffin tins with cupcake liners and evenly spoon in prepared butter mixture.
4. Place muffin tins into the refrigerator for 1 hour or until firm.
5. Then place chocolate in a small heatproof bowl and microwave for 45 seconds or more until melted.
6. Stir until smooth and then spoon this mixture over butter cups, spreading to the edges.
7. Freeze cups more for 15 to 30 minutes or until set.
8. Serve straight away or store in the freezer.

Raspberry Coconut Bark Fat Bombs

Servings: 12
Total time: 1 hour and 10 minutes;

Nutrition Value:

Calories: 234 Cal, Carbs: 6.5 g, Fat: 23.5 g, Protein: 1.7 g, Fiber: 4.1 g.

Ingredients:

- 1/2 cup dried raspberries, frozen
- 1/2 cup shredded coconut, unsweetened
- 1/4 cup powdered swerve sweetener
- 1/2 cup coconut oil
- 1/2 cup coconut butter

Method:

1. Place berries in a grinder and process at high speed or until a fine powder.
2. Place a saucepan over medium heat, add remaining ingredients, stir well and cook for 3 minutes or more until melted and combined, stirring frequently.
3. Take 8 by 8-inch baking pan, line with parchment paper, then pour half of the prepared mixture in it and spread evenly.
4. Add raspberry powder into the remaining mixture and dollop on mixture in the pan.
5. Swirl with knife and place pan into the refrigerator for 1 hour or more until set and firm.
6. Break into chunks and serve.

Chapter9: Frozen Desserts

Raspberry Sorbet

Servings: 8
Total time: 12 hours and 5 minutes;

Nutrition Value:

Calories: 43 Cal, Carbs: 5 g, Fat: 0 g, Protein: 1 g, Fiber: 3 g.

Ingredients:

- 1 ½ cups raspberries
- 1/4 cup erythritol sweetener
- 2 tablespoons gelatin
- 1 cup water

Method:

1. Place all the ingredients in a blender and puree until smooth.
2. Pass the mixture through a strainer into a freezer bag, about 1 quart, and place in freezer for 4 hours until thickened, massaging every hour.
3. Then freeze for 6 to 8 hours or until completely firm.
4. When ready to serve, remove the bag from the freezer, thaw for 10 minutes at room temperature and then scoop into serving bowls.

Saffron Pannacotta

Servings: 6
Total time: 2 hours and 10 minutes;

Nutrition Value:

Calories: 271 Cal, Carbs: 2 g, Fat: 29 g, Protein: 3 g, Fiber: 0 g.

Ingredients:

- ½ tablespoon gelatin
- 1 tablespoon swerve sweetener
- ¼ teaspoon vanilla extract, unsweetened
- 1/16 teaspoon saffron
- 2 cups heavy whipping cream, full-fat
- Water as needed
- 1 tablespoon chopped almonds, toasted

Method:

1. Place gelatin in a small bowl and stir in small amount of water according to instructions on the pack, or 1 tablespoon water for 1 teaspoon of gelatin and set aside until bloom.
2. In the meantime, place a small saucepan over medium heat, add remaining ingredients except for almonds, stir well and bring the mixture to a light boil.
3. Then lower heat and simmer mixture for 3 minutes or until mixture begin to thicken.
4. Remove pan from heat, stir in gelatin until dissolved completely and divide the mixture evenly between six ramekins.
5. Cover ramekins with plastic wrap and chill in the refrigerator for 2 hours.
6. When ready to serve, top with toasted almonds and serve.

Chocolate-Covered Macadamia Nut Fat Bombs

Servings: 4
Total time: 40 minutes;

Nutrition Value:

Calories: 161 Cal, Carbs: 4 g, Fat: 16 g, Protein: 2 g, Fiber: 2 g.

Ingredients:

- 1 ½ ounce macadamia nuts halves
- ¼ cup chocolate chips, stevia-sweetened
- 1/8 teaspoon sea salt and more as needed
- 1 tablespoon avocado oil

Method:

1. Place chocolate chips in a heatproof bowl and microwave for 50 to 60 seconds or until melted.
2. Stir chocolate, and then stir in salt and oil until blended.
3. Take 8 mini muffin cups, place three nuts into each cup and then evenly spoon prepared chocolate mixture, covering nuts completely.
4. Sprinkle with more salt and chill in the freezer for 30 minutes or more until solid.
5. Serve straightaway or store in a plastic bag into the freezer.

Lemon Ice Cream

Servings: 6
Total time: 5 minutes;

Nutrition Value:

Calories: 269 Cal, Carbs: 3 g, Fat: 27 g, Protein: 5 g, Fiber: 0 g.

Ingredients:

- 1 lemon, juiced and zested
- 1/3 cup erythritol sweetener
- 3 eggs
- 1 ¾ cups heavy whipping cream, full-fat and unsweetened

Method:

1. Separate egg yolks and white in two bowls and beat egg whites with an electric beater until stiff peaks form.
2. Add sweetener to egg yolks and whisk until light and fluffy.
3. Then stir in lemon juice and fold egg yolks into egg white.
4. Place cream in another bowl and whip well until soft peaks form.
5. Place the bowl in the freezer and freeze for 2 hours or until ice cream reach to the desired consistency, stirring every half an hour.
6. When ready to serve, thaw ice cream for 15 minutes at room temperature and then scoop into serving bowls.

Vanilla Panna Cotta

Servings: 4
Total time: 3 hours and 15 minutes;

Nutrition Value:

Calories: 422 Cal, Carbs: 4 g, Fat: 43 g, Protein: 4 g, Fiber: 0 g.

Ingredients:

- 2 tablespoons pomegranate seeds
- 1 teaspoon erythritol sweetener
- 2 teaspoons gelatin
- 1 tablespoon vanilla extract, unsweetened
- 2 cups heavy whipping cream, full-fat
- Water as needed

Method:

1. Place gelatin in a small bowl and stir in small amount of water according to instructions on the pack, or 1 tablespoon water for 1 teaspoon of gelatin and set aside until bloom.
2. In the meantime, place a saucepan over medium heat, add sweetener, vanilla, and cream and bring to boil.
3. Then lower heat to medium-low level and simmer mixture for 3 to 4 minutes or until mixture begins to thicken.
4. Remove pan from heat, stir in gelatin until dissolved completely and then evenly divide between 4 ramekins.
5. Cool ramekins at room temperature, then cover with plastic wrap and chill in the refrigerator for 2 to 3 hours.
6. When ready to serve, thaw pannacotta at room temperature, then top with pomegranate seeds and serve.

Chocolate Avocado Ice Cream

Servings: 8
Total time: 5 minutes;

Nutrition Value:

Calories: 289 Cal, Carbs: 14 g, Fat: 85 g, Protein: 1 g, Fiber: 6 g.

Ingredients:

- 2 medium avocados, pitted and peeled
- 1/3 cup erythritol sweetener
- 1/8 teaspoon stevia
- 1/2 cup cocoa powder, unsweetened
- 2 teaspoons vanilla extract, unsweetened
- 1 cup coconut milk, unsweetened and full-fat
- 1/2 cup coconut cream

Method:

1. Place all the ingredients in a food processor and pulse at high speed for 1 to 2 minutes or until smooth.
2. Then tip the mixture into a bowl, place it in the freezer and freeze for 2 hours or until ice cream reach to the desired consistency, stirring every half an hour.
3. When ready to serve, thaw ice cream for 15 minutes at room temperature and then scoop into serving bowls.

Mint and Chocolate Chip Ice Bombs

Servings: 14

Total time: 3 hours and 10 minutes;

Nutrition Value:

Calories: 67 Cal, Carbs: 2.8 g, Fat: 6 g, Protein: 0.5 g, Fiber: 1.1 g.

Ingredients:

- 1 medium avocado, pitted and peeled
- 2.1-ounce dark chocolate, chopped
- 1/4 cup and 1 tablespoon erythritol sweetener
- 1 teaspoon peppermint extract
- 1 cup coconut milk, unsweetened and full-fat

Method:

1. Place all the ingredients, except for chocolate, in a food processor and pulse for 1 to 2 minutes at high speed or until smooth.
2. Tip the mixture in a bowl and fold in chocolate until mixed.
3. Divide the mixture evenly between 14 candy molds or round cake mold and freeze for 2 to 3 hours or until set and firm.
4. Serve when ready.

Tiramisu Ice Bombs

Servings: 12
Total time: 3 hours and 15 minutes;

Nutrition Value:

Calories: 25 Cal, Carbs: 0.9 g, Fat: 2.3 g, Protein: 0.2 g, Fiber: 0.2 g.

Ingredients:

For the Ice Bombs:

- 1/4 cup erythritol sweetener
- 2 teaspoons rum extract, unsweetened
- 1/4 cup strong brewed coffee, chilled
- 1 1/4 cups coconut milk, full-fat and unsweetened

For the Coating:

- 1 ¼ tablespoon chocolate
- 1 tablespoon cacao butter

Method:

1. Place all the ingredients for ice bombs in a food processor and pulse at high speed for 1 to 2 minutes or until smooth and creamy.
2. Divide the mixture evenly between 12 candy molds or round cake mold and freeze for 2 to 3 hours or until set and firm.
3. When ready to serve, place chocolate and cacao butter in a heatproof bowl and microwave for 45 seconds or more until melted and stir well.
4. Pierce each frozen ice bomb with a toothpick and coat with melted chocolate completely and place on a parchment lined a baking tray.
5. Place tray into the freezer for 15 minutes or more until harden.
6. Serve straight away or store in plastic bag in the freezer.

Chapter 10: Custard and Mousse

Buttercream

Servings: 4
Total time: 10 minutes;

Nutrition Value:

Calories: 412 Cal, Carbs: 2 g, Fat: 46 g, Protein: 1 g, Fiber: 1 g.

Ingredients:

- 2 teaspoons erythritol sweetener
- 1½ teaspoon ground cinnamon
- 2 teaspoons vanilla extract, unsweetened
- 8-ounce softened butter, unsalted

Method:

1. Place a small saucepan over medium heat, add ¼ of butter and cook for 4 to 5 minutes or until butter turns into amber color, don't burn it.
2. Transfer browned butter into a large bowl and then use a hand mixer to beat in remaining ingredients, one at a time, until fluffy.
3. Taste to adjust sweetness and serve straightaway.

Berry Mousse

Servings: 8
Total time: 3 hours and 5 minutes;

Nutrition Value:

Calories: 260 Cal, Carbs: 5 g, Fat: 27 g, Protein: 3 g, Fiber: 2 g.

Ingredients:

- 2 ounce chopped pecans
- 3-ounce fresh strawberries
- ½ of a lemon, zested
- ¼ teaspoon vanilla extract, unsweetened
- 2 cups heavy whipping cream, full-fat

Method:

1. Place cream in a large bowl and whip using an electric beater until soft peaks form.
2. Beat in lemon zest and vanilla, then add berries and pecans and stir well.
3. Cover bowl with plastic wrap and place in refrigerator for 3 hours.
4. Serve when ready.

Vanilla Custard

Servings: 4
Total time: 1 hour and 10 minutes;

Nutrition Value:

Calories: 215 Cal, Carbs: 1 g, Fat: 21 g, Protein: 4 g, Fiber: 0 g.

Ingredients:

- 1 teaspoon erythritol sweetener
- 1 teaspoon vanilla extract, unsweetened
- ¼ cup melted coconut oil
- 6 egg yolks
- ½ cup almond milk, unsweetened and full-fat

Method:

1. Place vanilla in a large bowl, add sweetener, yolks, and milk and whisk with an electric beater until smooth and then slowly whisk in oil.
2. Place a saucepan, half full with water, over medium-high heat, and bring the water to simmer.
3. Then place the bowl containing egg yolks mixture and constantly whisk for 5 minutes or until thickened and food thermometer read 140 degrees F for 3 minutes.
4. When done, remove custard from the water bath and let chill for 1 hour before serving.

Gingerbread Crème Brûlée

Servings: 6
Total time: 1 hour;

Nutrition Value:

Calories: 274 Cal, Carbs: 3 g, Fat: 28 g, Protein: 4 g, Fiber: 0 g.

Ingredients:

- 2 tablespoons erythritol sweetener
- 2 teaspoons pumpkin pie spice
- ¼ teaspoon vanilla extract, unsweetened
- 4 egg yolks
- 1 ¾ cups heavy whipping cream, full-fat

Method:

1. Set oven to 360 degrees F and let preheat.
2. In the meantime, place egg yolks in a bowl, then whisk well and set aside.
3. Place a medium saucepan over medium heat, add cream and bring to boil.
4. Then stir in sweetener, pumpkin pie spice, and vanilla until smooth.
5. Slowly whisk this mixture into yolks until combined, then pour evenly between six ovenproof ramekins and nestled them in a baking dish or casserole.
6. Pour water into the baking dish about halfway up to ramekins and place the baking dish into the oven.
7. Bake for 30 minutes or until top is nicely brown.
8. When done, transfer ramekins to wire rack and let cool completely.
9. Serve straightaway.

Egg Custard

Servings: 6
Total time: 1 hour and 40 minutes;

Nutrition Value:

Calories: 319 Cal, Carbs: 3 g, Fat: 32 g, Protein: 5 g, Fiber: 0 g.

Ingredients:

- 1/4 teaspoon salt
- 1/2 teaspoon ground cinnamon
- 1/4 cup swerve sweetener
- 1 tablespoon vanilla extract, unsweetened
- 3 eggs
- 2 cups heavy whipping cream, full-fat

Method:

1. Set oven to 350 degrees F and let preheat.
2. In the meantime, place a kettle filled with water over medium heat and bring to boil.
3. Crack eggs in a medium bowl and whisk well until foamy.
4. Then whisk in salt, cinnamon, sweetener, vanilla, and cream until mixed and then divide evenly between six custard cups.
5. Place custard cups in a baking dish or large casserole and then pour boiling water into it, about 1-inch up to the cups.
6. Place casserole into the oven and bake for 30 minutes or until inserted skewer into the center of custard comes out clean.
7. When done, transfer custard cups to a wire rack and cool completely.
8. Serve straightaway.

Coconut Cream Custard

Servings: 6
Total time: 4 hours and 10 minutes;

Nutrition Value:

Calories: 217 Cal, Carbs: 1 g, Fat: 21 g, Protein: 3 g, Fiber: 0 g.

Ingredients:

- 1/8 teaspoon sea salt
- 2 tablespoons erythritol sweetener
- 1/8 teaspoon stevia
- 1 1/4 teaspoons vanilla extract, unsweetened
- 1 1/4 teaspoon coconut extract, unsweetened
- 4 tablespoons shredded coconut, unsweetened
- 8 egg yolks
- 1 cup heavy cream, full-fat
- 1/2 cup water

Method:

1. Place egg yolks in a bowl and whisk until smooth.
2. Place a medium saucepan over medium heat, add salt, sweetener, stevia, water, and cream and whisk until combined.
3. Heat the mixture until mixture starts to steamed, whisking frequently, and then slowly whisk ½ cup of this mixture until combined.
4. Add the egg yolks mixture into the pan, whisk well and bring to a gentle boil, whisking constantly.
5. Continue boiling for another minute or until thicken and then whisk in remaining ingredients.
6. Pour the mixture evenly between six custard bowls and let cool at room temperature.

7. Then cover each custard bowl with plastic wrap and chill in the refrigerator for 3 to 4 hours.
8. Garnish with coconut and serve.

Lemon Meringue Custard

Servings: 4
Total time: 2 hours and 20 minutes;

Nutrition Value:

Calories: 353.8 Cal, Carbs: 4.7 g, Fat: 35.4 g, Protein: 4.9 g, Fiber: 2 g.

Ingredients:

For the Custard:

- ½ teaspoon xanthan gum
- 1/8 teaspoon salt
- 1/3 cup erythritol sweetener
- 2 lemons, zested
- ½ teaspoon vanilla extract, unsweetened
- ½ teaspoon lemon extract, unsweetened
- 1 ½ cups heavy whipping cream, full-fat
- 2 egg yolks

For the Meringue:

- 1 tablespoon erythritol sweetener
- 1/8 teaspoon vanilla extract, unsweetened
- 2 egg whites
- 1/8 teaspoon cream of tartar

Method:

1. Prepare custard and for this, place a medium saucepan over low heat and add xanthan gum, salt, sweetener and lemon zest.
2. Stir well, then whisk in cream, 2 tablespoons at a time, until thoroughly combined.

3. Whisk in eggs, then switch heat to medium-low level and bring to simmer, stirring frequently.
4. Remove pan from heat, add extracts and divide custard between four ramekins.
5. Prepare meringue right away and for this, place eggs in a bowl, add cream of tartar and whip using a stand mixer until soft peaks form.
6. Whisk in sweetener and vanilla until stiff peaks form and spoon the mixture evenly on top of custard completely.
7. Create peaks on meringue by pressing a spoon into it and lifting it upward.
8. Place top rack of oven about 8-inches away from the heating element of broiler and turn to high heat.
9. Place ramekins into a cookie sheet and place on the top rack.
10. Cook for 40 seconds, turning cookie sheet halfway, until meringue is nicely brown, don't over-brown.
11. When done, transfer ramekins to the refrigerator and let cool for 2 hours before serving.

Eggnog Custard

Servings: 8
Total time: 2 hours and 10 minutes;

Nutrition Value:

Calories: 122 Cal, Carbs: 1 g, Fat: 11 g, Protein: 3 g, Fiber: 0 g.

Ingredients:

- 1/4 cup erythritol sweetener
- 1/4 teaspoon ground nutmeg
- 4 eggs
- 1 cup half and half
- 1/2 cup heavy whipping cream, full-fat

Method:

1. Place eggs in a bowl and blend using an electric beater at low speed until beaten.
2. Beat in remaining ingredients, one at a time, and then divide mixture between 6 heatproof glass bowls.
3. Place these bowls into a microwave oven and cook for 4 minutes at 50 percent power.
4. Then stir well and continue cooking for 3 to 4 minutes at 50 percent power.
5. Stir well, let the custard cool completely and then serve.

Conclusion

Ketogenic Diet is called a miracle diet, and indeed, it is a miracle due to its amazing diet plan that provides incredible benefits to the body and improves health. Hence, a common misconception Keto have that they cannot have sweets or their favorite dessert. You can eat any of your favorite desserts on Keto. All you have to do is to make sure that your body is in the ketosis state and you can ensure this by using ingredients are whole foods and Keto-friendly sweeteners.

This e-book will enable you to learn how to satisfy your sweet craving while being on Keto. Moreover, it will make you proficient in converting your car and sugar filled desserts into high-fat decadents. You can even make your collection of Ketogenic desserts.